Andreas Capellanus

THE ART OF COURTLY LOVE

Translated by
JOHN JAY PARRY

Edited and abridged by
FREDERICK W. LOCKE
Stanford University

FREDERICK UNGAR PUBLISHING CO.
NEW YORK

MILESTONES
OF THOUGHT
in the History of Ideas

General Editor
F. W. STROTHMANN
Stanford University

Tenth Printing, 1971

Printed in the United States of America

ISBN 0-8044-6075-2

Library of Congress Catalog Card Number 56-12400

INTRODUCTION

Andreas Capellanus and the Doctrine of Courtly Love

MUCH HAS happened to change our views of the Middle Ages since the publication of Will Durant's *History of Philosophy*. It will be recalled that in his first edition Mr. Durant saw fit to pass over medieval philosophy as completely unworthy of serious examination. In doing so he was illustrating most eloquently the prevalent attitude towards the ten centuries which had been hidden away in shame between Antiquity and Modernity. And though at this late date it would be almost impossible to change the name, the term "Middle Ages" itself has had no small influence upon our conception of a vast period of European history which has not been so homogeneous as we had been led to believe.

Today the situation is quite different. There is at the present time a very lively interest in the Middle Ages, a growing awareness of the significance of its contributions to literature, art, music, and thought. It is no longer possible to characterize the period between 500 and 1500 as the Dark Ages. There has been, indeed, much talk in recent years of a Renaissance of the Twelfth Century, a kind of proto-renaissance, wherein are to be detected symptoms of that intellectual and artistic unrest which culminated in the High Renaissance of the sixteenth century. All of our large universities offer courses in Medieval Latin and the vernacular languages and literatures of the older period. There has also been a renewed interest in the study of Dante and the Troubadours, and through the work of such scholars as Étienne Gilson there has come about such an interest in medieval philosophy that at least one American university

has at this time a chair devoted to this subject. In the area
of medieval art the books of Emile Mâle and Joan Evans
have awakened a new kind of appreciation and understand-
ing of Romanesque and Gothic style.

The publication of the treatise of Andreas Capellanus
in the "Milestones of Thought" series requires, therefore,
no defense. The work itself, however, may stand in need of
certain background information which will better enable the
reader to gain a very necessary perspective.

In the eyes of Capellanus, passionate love is an ennobling force. As a matter of fact, it is the source of all
manly virtues. This view of passionate love between the
sexes is alien to the Greeks and the Romans. Whenever
passionate love manifests itself in the literature of Antiquity,
it is either regarded as a chastisement inflicted on men by
the gods—as in Euripides, to whom the love of Phaedra for
Hippolytus is a punishment visited upon the young man for
his neglect of Aphrodite—or, as in the case of Ovid, it is
viewed simply as sensual gratification.

When, therefore, Capellanus, expressing the ideals of
the social group to which he belonged, depicts passionate
love as an ennobling experience, we must recognize this
evaluation as something totally new; and from a social point
of view we must even recognize it as revolutionary. For when
a passionate lover obediently subjects himself to the beloved
lady as to his "mistress," he grants to this lady a status
which women simply did not enjoy either in Antiquity or
in the early Middle Ages.

In spite of the Christian form of society, it would be
misleading indeed to conceive of a status for women during
the early Middle Ages which was at all comparable to that
of the modern American woman. Women are not important,
for instance, in the old French Epics. In the eyes of medieval men, this is a man's world, and it is only the deeds of
men, particularly of warriors, that are worthy of being
chronicled. Unless a woman in the older period happens to
be a saint, she is not mentioned at any length; and there is

no concern with passionate love between the sexes, but rather, as in Antiquity, with the friendship of man for man, of warrior for warrior, as classically illustrated in the devotion of Roland and Olivier for each other in "The Song of Roland."

Outside of marriage, women might be used to alleviate concupiscence; and in the married state, recommended by St. Paul because it is better to marry than to burn, she had the additional function of being a childbearer and a housekeeper, hardly that of a companion with a status equal to that of men. From the very earliest period of Christianity, passionate love was deplored; and not until the time of Albertus Magnus and Thomas Aquinas in the thirteenth century did the theologians begin to mitigate their contention that passionate love towards even one's wife was sinful.

Behind this medieval attitude towards women was a monastic tradition whose influence upon letters and institutions cannot be overestimated. The angry denunciation against the perennial Eve is a cry that is heard throughout the period: every woman is *Eva rediviva,* the personification of the temptress through whom man originally fell from innocence.

According to the record, a new conception of love appeared at the beginning of the twelfth century, a conception which was eventually to change the prevalent attitude toward women. This new attitude showed itself at first exclusively among the members of the aristocratic class in the south of France, and even when it moved north there is no indication that it was responsible for any marked change in attitude within the lower classes of society. The initial symptoms of this change in the aristocracy's attitude toward love are noticed in the south of France in the person of Guillaume IX, duke of Poitiers (1071-1127), who is the first of the known Troubadours. But it is not until we come to Bernart de Ventadorn (1148-1195) that the radically new theme of Provençal lyric poetry, i.e., Courtly Love, manifests its real character.

The term *amour courtois,* or Courtly Love, is of modern origin. It was first applied in 1883 by the great French medievalist Gaston Paris in an attempt to coin a term for this new form of love which makes such a decided break with previous forms and which appears for the first time in Europe among the Troubadours of Provence.

The poetry of the Troubadours and that of the Trouvères in the north of France speaks of a love which, while essentially adulterous, inspires the man with nobility of character and offers him, through the beloved, a transcendent experience. It is this power of transformation which, more than anything else, constitutes the distinguishing characteristic of Courtly Love, a love which both as a literary theme and as a social ideal is something entirely new on the European scene, and from which our modern notions of romantic love derive in a large measure. Without Courtly Love, the tragic passionate love of the modern novel and theatre would be difficult to explain. Courtly Love has influenced men's deepest attitude toward the other sex, our unquestioned sense of courtesy in the West, our persistent, if socially crystallized, deference toward women. Courtly Love is also responsible for the "democratization" of relations between man and woman, inasmuch as not social position but intrinsic worth determined the mutual acceptability of the partners according to the courtly code.

Though scholars have traced many of the lines of transmission of Troubadour poetry and have shown most clearly the sources of many of the forms of Provençal verse, the origins of the phenomenon of Courtly Love still remain wrapped in mystery. Up to the present, there is no agreement as to how it actually started or whence it derives. Attempts have been made to find its origins in Ovid, in Arabic philosophy, in Neo-Platonism, in the mystical writings of Christians and Moslems, and in the heresy of the Albigensians.

Whatever may be the origin of what has come to be called Courtly Love, it is the codification of its principles that is the subject of *The Art of Courtly Love* (*De arte honeste amandi*), written some time between 1174 and 1186 by Andreas Capellanus. His work, like that of the *Art Poétique* of Boileau, which appeared after the classical movement of the seventeenth century had come to flower, is descriptive, not prescriptive: it does not propose anything new, but rather codifies what was already in existence.

There are also signs that its author cannot accept the code he sets forth. The evidence for this is in the strange Third Book which flatly contradicts the principles set up in the first two. Is this third book an apology offered by the Christian conscience because of the unacceptability of Courtly Love? We do not know.

Only one thing is certain. As a description of the theory of Courtly Love, *The Art of Courtly Love* is an invaluable document and among the most provocative which have come down from the period of the High Middle Ages.

F.W.L.

SELECTED BIBLIOGRAPHY

Andreae Capellani regii Francorum De amore libri tres.
Recensuit E. Trojel. Havniae [Copenhagen] in Libraria
Gandiana, 1892.

Andreae Capellani regii Francorum De amore libri tres.
Text llatí publicat per Amadeu Pagès. Castelló de la
Plana [Sociedad Castellonense de Cultura], 1929.

Denomy, A. J. *The Heresy of Courtly Love*. New York:
Macmillan Company, 1947.

Lewis, C. S. *The Allegory of Love*. London: Oxford University Press, 1948.

NOTE

The translation from which this text has been edited is that of the late Professor John Jay Parry, *The Art of Courtly Love*, Columbia University Press, 1941. Changes have been made in Professor Parry's translation only at those points where new connections had to be established through the excerpting of material, or when it was deemed advisable to emend a colloquial expression which is not any more current. For the use of Professor Parry's translation we acknowledge the kind permission of Columbia University Press.

The chapter numbering of the Parry edition has been changed to conform with the sequence of the selections here presented.

CONTENTS

BOOK THREE

The Rejection of Love

AUTHOR'S PREFACE

I am greatly impelled by the continual urging of my love for you, my revered friend Walter, to make known by word of mouth and to teach you by my writings the way in which a state of love between two lovers may be kept unharmed and likewise how those who do not love may get rid of the darts of Venus that are fixed in their hearts.

You tell me that you are a new recruit of Love, and, having recently been wounded by an arrow of his, you do not know how to manage your horse's reins properly and you cannot find any cure for yourself. How serious this is and how it troubles my soul no words of mine can make clear to you. For I know, having learned from experience, that it does not do the man who owes obedience to Venus's service any good to give careful thought to anything except how he may always be doing something that will entangle him more firmly in his chains; he thinks he has nothing good except what may wholly please his love.

Therefore, although it does not seem expedient to devote oneself to things of this kind or fitting for any prudent man to engage in this kind of hunting, nevertheless, because of the affection I have for you I can by no means refuse your request; because I know clearer than day that after you have learned the art of love your progress in it will be more cautious, in so far as I can I shall comply with your desire.

BOOK ONE

Introduction to the Treatise on Love

We must first consider what love is, whence it gets its name, what the effect of love is, between what persons love may exist, how it may be acquired, retained, increased, decreased, and ended, what are the signs that one's love is returned, and what one of the lovers ought to do if the other is unfaithful.

CHAPTER I

What Love Is

Love is a certain inborn suffering derived from the sight of and excessive meditation upon the beauty of the opposite sex, which causes each one to wish above all things the embraces of the other and by common desire to carry out all of love's precepts in the other's embrace.

That love is suffering is easy to see, for before the love becomes equally balanced on both sides there is no torment greater, since the lover is always in fear that his love may not gain its desire and that he is wasting his efforts. He fears, too, that rumors of it may get abroad, and he fears everything that might harm it in any way, for before things are perfected a slight disturbance often spoils them. If he is a poor man, he also fears that the woman may scorn his poverty; if he is ugly, he fears that she may despise his lack of beauty or may give her love to a more handsome man; if he is rich, he fears that his parsimony in the past may stand in his way. To tell the truth, no one can number the fears of one single lover. This kind of love, then, is a suffering which is felt by only one of the persons and may be called "single love." But even after both are in love the fears that arise are just as great, for each of the lovers fears that what he has acquired with so much effort may be lost through the effort of someone else, which is certainly much worse for a man than if, having no hope, he sees that his efforts are accomplishing nothing, for it is worse to lose the things you are seeking than to be deprived of a gain you merely hope for. The lover fears, too, that he may offend his loved one in some way; indeed he fears so many things that it would be difficult to tell them.

That this suffering is inborn I shall show you clearly, because if you will look at the truth and distinguish carefully you will see that it does not arise out of any action; only from the reflection of the mind upon what it sees does this suffering come. For when a man sees some woman fit for love and shaped according to his taste, he begins at once to lust after her in his heart; then the more he thinks about her the more he burns with love, until he comes to a fuller meditation. Presently he begins to think about the fashioning of the woman and to differentiate her limbs, to think about what she does, and to pry into the secrets of her body, and he desires to put each part of it to the fullest use. Then after he has come to this complete meditation, love cannot hold the reins, but he proceeds at once to action; straightway he strives to get a helper to find an intermediary. He begins to plan how he may find favor with her, and he begins to seek a place and a time opportune for talking; he looks upon a brief hour as a very long year, because he cannot do anything fast enough to suit his eager mind. It is well known that many things happen to him in this manner. This inborn suffering comes, therefore, from seeing and meditating. Not every kind of meditation can be the cause of love, an excessive one is required; for a restrained thought does not, as a rule, return to the mind, and so love cannot arise from it.

CHAPTER II

Between What Persons Love May Exist

Now, in love you should note first of all that love cannot exist except between persons of opposite sexes. Between two men or two women love can find no place, for we see that two persons of the same sex are not at all fitted for giving each other the exchanges of love or for practicing the acts natural to it. Whatever nature forbids, love is ashamed to accept.

CHAPTER III

What the Effect of Love Is

Now it is the effect of love that a true lover cannot be degraded with any avarice. Love causes a rough and uncouth man to be distinguished for his handsomeness; it can endow a man even of the humblest birth with nobility of character; it blesses the proud with humility; and the man in love becomes accustomed to performing many services gracefully for everyone. O what a wonderful thing is love, which makes a man shine with so many virtues and teaches everyone, no matter who he is, so many good traits of character! There is another thing about love that we should not praise in few words: it adorns a man, so to speak, with the virtue of chastity, because he who shines with the light of one love can hardly think of embracing another woman, even a beautiful one. For when he thinks deeply of his beloved the sight of any other woman seems to his mind rough and rude.

CHAPTER IV

What Persons Are Fit for Love

We must now see what persons are fit to bear the arms of love. You should know that everyone of sound mind who is capable of doing the work of Venus may be wounded by one of love's arrows unless prevented by age, or blindness, or excess of passion.

An excess of passion is a bar to love, because there are men who are slaves to such passionate desire that they cannot be held in the bonds of love—men who, after they have thought long about some woman or even enjoyed her, when they see another woman straightway desire her embraces, and they forget about the services they have received from their first love and they feel no gratitude for them. Men of this kind lust after every woman they see; their love is like that of a shameless dog. They should rather, I believe, be compared to asses, for they are moved only by that low nature which shows that men are on the level of the other animals rather than by that true nature which sets us apart from all the other animals by the difference of reason.

CHAPTER V

In What Manner Love May Be Acquired,
and in How Many Ways

It remains next to be seen in what ways love may be acquired.

A beautiful figure wins love with very little effort, especially when the lover who is sought is simple, for a simple lover thinks that there is nothing to look for in one's beloved besides a beautiful figure and face and a body well cared for.

But a wise woman will seek as a lover a man of praiseworthy character—not one who anoints himself all over like a woman or makes a rite of the care of the body, for it does not go with a masculine figure to adorn oneself in womanly fashion or to be devoted to the care of the body.

Likewise, if you see a woman too heavily rouged you will not be taken in by her beauty unless you have already discovered that she is good company besides, since a woman who puts all her reliance on her rouge usually doesn't have any particular gifts of character. As I said about men, so with women—I believe you should not seek for beauty so much as for excellence of character. For since all of us human beings are derived originally from the same stock and all naturally claim the same ancestor, it was not beauty or care of the body or even abundance of possessions, but excellence of character alone which first made a distinction of nobility among men and led to the difference of class.

Character alone, then, is worthy of the crown of love. Many times fluency of speech will incline to love the hearts of those who do not love, for an elaborate line of talk on the part of the lover usually sets love's arrows a-flying and creates a presumption in favor of the excellent character of the speaker. How this may be I shall try to show you as briefly as I can.

To this end I shall first explain to you that one woman belongs to the middle class, a second to the simple nobility, and a third to the higher nobility. So it is with men: one is of the middle class, another of the nobility, a third of the higher nobility, and a fourth of the very highest nobility. What I mean by a woman of the middle class is clear enough to you; a noblewoman is one descended from an untitled nobleman [vavasor] or a lord, or is the wife of one of these, while a woman of the higher nobility is descended from great lords. The same rules apply to men, except that a man married to a woman of higher or lower rank than himself does not change his rank. A married woman changes her status to match that of her husband, but a man can never change his nobility by marriage. In addition, among men we find one rank more than among women, since there is a man more noble than any of these, that is, the clerk.

FIRST DIALOGUE

A man of the middle class speaks with a woman
of the same class.

THE MAN SAYS: "When the Divine Being made you there was nothing that He left undone. I know that there is no defect in your beauty, none in your good sense, none in you at all except, it seems to me, that you have enriched no one by your love. I marvel greatly that Love permits so beautiful and so sensible a woman to serve for long outside his camp. If you should take service with Love, blessed above all others will that man be whom you shall crown with your love! Now if I, by my merits, might be worthy of such an honor, no lover in the world could really be compared with me."

THE WOMAN SAYS: "You seem to be lying, since although I do not have a beautiful figure you extol me as beautiful beyond all other women and although I lack the ornament of wisdom you praise my good sense. The very highest wisdom ought not to be required of a woman descended from the middle class."

THE MAN SAYS: "It is a habit of wise people never to admit with their own mouths their good looks or their good character, and by so doing they clearly show their character, because prudent people guard their words so carefully that no one may have reason to apply to them that common proverb which runs, 'All praise is filthy in one's own mouth.' You, like a wise woman, not wishing to fall foul of this saying, leave all praise of you to others; but there are so many who do praise you that it would never be right to say that one of them meant to lie. Even those who do not love

you for the sake of your family are, I know, diligent in sing-
ing your praises. And besides, if you think you are not
beautiful, you should believe that I must really be in love,
since to me your beauty excels that of all other women; and
love makes even an ugly woman seem very beautiful to her
lover. You said, too, that you come of a humble family.
But this shows that you are much more deserving of praise
and blessed with greater nobility, since yours does not come
from your descent or from your ancestors, but good character and good manners alone have given to you a more
worthy kind of nobility. In the beginning the same nature
created all men, and to this day they would have remained
equal had not greatness of soul and worth of character com-
menced to set men apart from each other by the inequality
of nobility."

THE WOMAN SAYS: "If I am as noble as you are trying
to make out, you, being a man of the middle class, should
seek the love of some woman of the same class, while I
look for a noble lover to match my noble status; for nobility
and commonalty do not go well together or dwell in the
same abode."

THE MAN SAYS: "Your answer would seem good enough
if it were only in women that a lowly birth might be en-
nobled by excellence of character. But since an excellent
character makes noble not only women but men also, you
are perhaps wrong in refusing me your love, since my manners, too, may illumine me with the virtue of nobility. Your
first concern should be whether I lack refined manners, and
if you find my status higher than you would naturally ex-
pect, you ought not deprive me of the hope of your love.
For one whose nobility is that of character it is more proper
to choose a lover whose nobility is of the same kind than
one who is high-born but unmannerly. Indeed, if you should
find a man who is distinguished by both kinds of nobility,
it would be better to take as a lover the man whose only
nobility is that of character. For the one gets his nobility
from his ancient stock and from his noble father and derives

it as a sort of inheritance from those from whom he gets his being; but the other gets his nobility only from himself, and what he takes is not derived from his family tree, but springs only from the best qualities of his mind. You should therefore approve the second man's nobility more than that of the other. For I notice that we consider more worthy of praise and reward that king who received a small realm from his ancestors and afterwards by his virtuous rule brought countless nations under his sway than the king who retains undisturbed the many kingdoms which he inherited. If, therefore, you recognize that I enjoy nobility of manners, incline your excellence toward me and give me at least the hope of your love, which I have so long desired, so that I may live; for there is no hope of saving me if you cause me to despair of your love."

SECOND DIALOGUE

A man of the middle class speaks with a woman of the nobility.

THE MAN SAYS: "I know well that Love is not in the habit of differentiating men with titles of distinction, but that he obligates all equally to serve in his army, making no exceptions for beauty or birth and making no distinctions of sex or of inequality of family, considering only this, whether anybody is fit to bear Love's armor. Love is a thing that copies Nature herself, and so lovers ought to make no more distinction between classes of men than Love himself does. Just as love inflames men of all classes, so lovers should draw no distinctions of rank, but consider only whether the man who asks for love has been wounded by Love. Supported by this unanswerable argument, I may select for my beloved any woman I choose so long as I have no depravity of character to debase me."

THE WOMAN SAYS: "Who are you that ask for such great gifts? I know well enough what you look like, and the family you come from is obvious. But where can one find greater effrontery than in a man who for the space of a whole week devotes all his efforts to the various gains of business and then on the seventh day, his day of rest, tries to enjoy the gifts of love and to dishonor Love's commands and confound the distinctions of classes established among men from of old? It is not without cause or reason that this distinction of rank has been found among men from the very beginning; it is so that every man will stay within the bounds of his own class and be content with all things therein and never presume to arrogate to himself the things that were naturally set aside as belonging to a higher class, but will leave them severely alone. Who are you, then, to try to defile such ancient statutes and under the pretense of love to attempt to subvert the precepts of our ancestors and so presumptuously go beyond the limits of your own class?"

THE MAN SAYS: "Although I am repulsed by what you say, still as long as I live I shall not give up the idea of your love, because even if I am never to get the result I hope for, the mere hope I have gained from the greatness of my heart will cause my body to lead a tranquil life, and ultimately, perhaps, God will put into your mind a cure for my pain."

THE WOMAN SAYS: "May God give you a reward suited to your effort."

THE MAN SAYS: "That word alone shows me that my hope is bearing fruit, and I pray to God that you may always be interested in the care of my health and that my sails may find a quiet haven."

THIRD DIALOGUE

*A man of the middle class speaks with
a woman of the higher nobility.*

If a man of the middle class seeks the love of a woman of the higher nobility, he ought to have a most excellent character, for in order that a man of this class may prove worthy of the love of a woman of the higher nobility he must be a man with innumerable good things to his credit, one whom uncounted good deeds extol. It would seem a very great shame and a cause of reproach for a noblewoman to pass over the upper and the intermediate ranks and take a lover from the lower class unless good character in overwhelming quantity makes up for the lack of nobility. For it would not seem unreasonable to any sensible people that one could find in the lowest class good and excellent men, worthy of the love of a woman of such high rank, while in the upper classes no worthy man could be found, but all had to be rejected as of inferior quality. This is what you are told by the general rule of the logicians, which says, "If what appears more present is not present, neither will that which is believed less be." A man of the middle class must therefore greatly excel in character all the men of the two noble classes in order to deserve the love of a woman of the higher nobility, for no matter how worthy any commoner may be, it seems very much out of place if a countess or a marchioness or any woman of the same or a higher rank gives her love to a man of the middle class, and even the lower classes look upon it as a lowering and a demeaning of herself. The first thing people will think is that she does it out of too great an abundance of passion (a thing which I shall show later is wholly reprehensible), unless the man's character is so well known as to remove the suspicion of that. Well, then, isn't it proper that a woman of the higher nobility should give her love to a commoner if she finds him excellent in every way? I answer that if she finds anyone in the classes above him who is more worthy or as worthy, she ought to prefer the love of that man; but if she doesn't find any such person in these classes, then she should not reject the commoner.

Therefore a man of the middle class may be chosen in love by a woman of the higher nobility if after long probation he is found to be worthy. In that case he may make some such speech as the following:

"It doesn't seem at all profitable to dwell very much

on the praise of your person, for your character and your beauty echo through widely separated parts of the world, and, furthermore, praise uttered in the presence of the person praised seems to have the appearance of clever flattery. For the present, then, it is my intention, and the principal object which brings me here to you, to offer you myself and my services and to beg earnestly that Your Grace may see fit to accept them. And I beseech God in heaven that of His grace He may grant me to do those things which are wholly pleasing to your desire."

THE WOMAN SAYS: "You seem to have a reasonable defense, but what good deeds glorify you, what sort of character makes you worthy to obtain what you ask, I have never heard. He who asks for the love of an honorable woman, especially one of the upper nobility, ought to be of great fame and of all courtliness; but of you lofty fame seems to be perfectly silent. First, therefore, you should strive to do such things as deserve the reward which you ask, so that your request may not be considered too impudent."

THE MAN SAYS: "The height of courtesy seems to be contained in your remarks, in which you are so clearly concerned that all my actions should be laudable. And so, since I see that you are thoroughly instructed in the art of love, I ask you to give me a lesson—that is, I ask that Your Grace may see fit to teach me those things that are specially demanded in love, those which make a man most worthy of being loved, because after I have been instructed I shall have no defense for any mistakes I make and no opportunity to excuse myself. Since all courtesy comes from the plentiful stream of Love and to this generous lord should be credited the beginning of all good deeds and the carrying out to the end of every good, and since I am still inexperienced in love and ignorant of the subject, it is no wonder that I know nothing of what he can do and that I urgently seek to be taught his precepts; because what anyone desires with all his mind he begs for vehemently and receives with eagerness."

THE WOMAN SAYS: "You seem to be upsetting the natural order and course of things, since first you ask for love and then you show yourself in every way unworthy of it by asking like a raw recruit to be trained in the science of love. But since it would seem to set a shameful precedent, one prompted by avarice, if those who have experience were to deny their lessons to those who have not and ask to be taught, you will without a doubt obtain the grant of our instruction; and if you will pay careful attention to our words, before you leave you will be fully informed on the subjects you ask about.

"Well then, the man who would be considered worthy to serve in Love's army must not be in the least avaricious, but very generous; he must, in fact, give generously to as many people as he can. When he sees that money is needed, especially by noblemen and men of character, and when he thinks that his gifts would be helpful to anybody, he ought not wait to be urged, for a gift made in answer to a request seems dearly bought.

"And if he has a lord, he should offer him due respect. He should utter no word of blasphemy against God and His saints; he should show himself humble to all and should stand ready to serve everybody. He ought never speak a word in disparagement of any man, since those who speak evil may not remain within the threshold of courtesy. He ought not utter falsehood in praise of the wicked, but he should if possible make them better by secret reproofs. If he thinks that they remain wholly incorrigible, he should consider them stiff-necked and banish them from his company lest he be considered, and rightly, a promoter and a sharer of the error. He ought never mock anyone, especially the wretched, and he should not be quarrelsome or ready to take part in disputes; but he should be, so far as possible, a composer of differences. In the presence of women he should be moderate about his laughter, because, according to Solomon's saying, too much laughter is a sign of foolishness; and clever women are in the habit of turning away fools and unwise men in contempt or of eluding them beautifully. Great prudence is necessary in the management of a love affair and diligence in all one does.

"He ought to frequent assemblies of great men and to visit great courts. He should be moderate about indulging in games of dice. He should gladly call to mind and take to heart the great deeds of the men of old. He ought to be courageous in battle and hardy against his enemies, wise, cautious, and clever.

"He should not be a lover of several women at the same time, but for the sake of one he should be a devoted servant of all.

"He should devote only a moderate amount of care to the adornment of his person and should show himself wise and tractable and pleasant to everybody, although some men have the idea that women like it very much if they utter foolish, almost crazy, remarks and act like madmen. "He should be careful, too, not to utter falsehoods and should take care not to talk too much or to keep silent too much. He should not be too quick and sudden about making promises, because the man who is good-natured about making promises will be slow to keep them, and the man who is too ready to make them gets little credit.

"He should not utter harmful or shameful or mocking words against God's clergy or monks or any person connected with a religious house, but should always and everywhere render them due honor with all his strength and with all his mind, for the sake of Him whose service they perform. He ought to go to church frequently and there listen gladly to those who are constantly celebrating the divine service, although some men very foolishly believe that the women like it if they despise everything connected with the Church. He ought to be truthful in everything he says and never envy any man's renown. I have presented to you briefly the main points. If you have listened attentively to them and will be careful to practice them, you will be found worthy to plead in the court of Love."

SEVENTH DIALOGUE

*A man of the higher nobility speaks with a
woman of the simple nobility.*

When a man of the higher nobility addresses a woman
of the simple nobility, let him use the same speeches that
a nobleman and a man of the higher nobility use with a
woman of the middle class, except that part dealing with the
commendation of birth, and he must not boast very much
of the fact that he is noble. In addition he might begin with
this formula:

"I ought to give God greater thanks than any other
living man in the whole world because it is now granted me
to see with my eyes what my soul has desired above all else
to see, and I believe that God has granted it to me because
of my great longing and because He has seen fit to hear
the prayers of my importunate supplication. For not an hour
of the day or night could pass that I did not earnestly pray
God to grant me the boon of seeing you near me in the
flesh. It is no wonder that I was driven by so great an im-
pulse to see you and was tormented by so great a desire,
since the whole world extols your virtue and your wisdom,
and in the farthest parts of the world courts are fed upon
the tale of your goodness just as though it were a sort of
tangible food. And now I know in very truth that a human
tongue is not able to tell the tale of your beauty and your
prudence or a human mind to imagine it. And so the mighty
desire, which I already had, of seeing you and serving you
has greatly increased and will increase still more."

THE WOMAN SAYS: "We are separated by too wide and
too rough an expanse of country to be able to offer each
other love's solaces or to find proper opportunities for meet-
ing. Lovers who live near together can cure each other of
the torments that come from love, can help each other in
their common sufferings, and can nourish their love by
mutual exchanges and efforts; those, however, who are far

apart cannot perceive each other's pains, but each one has to relieve his own trouble and cure his own torments. So it seems that our love should go no further, because Love's rule teaches us that the daily sight of each other makes lovers love more ardently, while I can see on the other hand that by reason of distance love decreases and fails, and therefore everybody should try to find a lover who lives near by."

THE MAN SAYS: "You are troubling yourself to say what seems to be against all reason, for all men know that if one gets easily what he desires he holds it cheap and what formerly he longed for with his whole heart he now considers worthless. On the other hand, whenever the possession of some good thing is postponed by the difficulty of getting it, we desire it more eagerly and put forth a greater effort to keep it. Therefore if one has difficulty in obtaining the embraces of one's lover and obtains them rarely, the lovers are bound to each other in more ardent chains of love and their souls are linked together in heavier and closer bonds of affection. For constancy is made perfect amid the waves that buffet it, and perseverance is clearly seen in adversities. Rest seems sweeter to a man who is wearied by many labors than to one who lives in continual idleness, and a new-found shade seems to offer more to one who is burdened by the heat than to one who has been constantly in air of a moderate temperature. It is not one of Love's rules, as you said it was, that when lovers seldom meet the strength of their love is weakened, since we find it false and misleading. Therefore you cannot properly refuse me your love with the excuse of the long and difficult distance between us, but you should gratify me rather than someone who lives near by; besides, it is easier to conceal a love affair when the lovers do not meet than when they converse frequently with each other."

THE WOMAN SAYS: "So far as hiding one's love goes, I do not think there is any choice between a distant lover and one who is present. If the lover proves to be wise and clever it doesn't matter whether he is far from his beloved or near her, he will so govern his actions and his will that no one can guess the secrets of their love; on the other hand a foolish lover, whether far or near, can never conceal the secrets of his love. Your argument must therefore fall before this most obvious one on the other side. Besides there is another fact, by no means trivial, which keeps me from loving you. I have a husband who is greatly distinguished by his nobility, his good breeding, and his good character, and it would be wicked for me to violate his bed or submit to the embraces of any other man, since I know that he loves me with his whole heart and I am bound to him with all the devotion of mine. The laws themselves bid me refrain from loving another man when I am blessed with such a reward for my love."

THE MAN SAYS: "I admit it is true that your husband is a very worthy man and that he is more blest than any man in the world because he has been worthy to have the joy of embracing Your Highness. But I am greatly surprised that you wish to misapply the term 'love' to that marital affection which husband and wife are expected to feel for each other after marriage, since everybody knows that love can have no place between husband and wife. They may be bound to each other by a great and immoderate affection, but their feeling cannot take the place of love, because it cannot fit under the true definition of love. For what is love but an inordinate desire to receive passionately a furtive and hidden embrace? But what embrace between husband and wife can be furtive, I ask you, since they may be said to belong to each other and may satisfy each other's desires without fear that anybody will object.

"But there is another reason why husband and wife cannot love each other and that is that the very substance of love, without which true love cannot exist—I mean jealousy —is in such a case very much frowned upon and they should avoid it like the pestilence; but lovers should always welcome it as the mother and the nurse of love. From this you may see clearly that love cannot possibly flourish between you and your husband. Therefore, since every woman of character ought to love, prudently, you can without doing yourself any harm accept the prayers of a suppliant and endow your suitor with your love."

THE WOMAN SAYS: "You are trying to take under your protection what all men from early times down have agreed to consider very reprehensible and to reject as hateful. For who can rightly commend envious jealousy or speak in favor of it, since jealousy is nothing but a shameful and evil suspicion of a woman? God forbid, therefore, that any worthy man should feel jealous about anyone, since this proves hostile to every prudent person and throughout the world is hated by everybody good. You are trying also, under cover of defining love, to condemn love between husband and wife, saying that their embraces cannot be furtive, since without fear that anyone may object they can fulfill each other's desires. But if you understood the definition correctly it could not interfere with love between husband and wife, for the expression 'hidden embraces' is simply an explanation in different words of the preceding one, and there seems to be no impossibility in husband and wife giving each other hidden embraces, even though they can do so without the least fear that anybody may raise an objection. Everyone should choose that love which may be fostered by security for continual embraces and, what is more, can be practiced every day without any sin. I ought therefore to choose a man to enjoy my embraces who can be to me both husband and lover, because, no matter what the definition of love may say, love seems to be nothing but a great desire to enjoy carnal pleasure with someone, and nothing prevents this feeling existing between husband and wife."

THE MAN SAYS: "If the theory of love were perfectly clear to you and Love's dart had ever touched you, your own feelings would have shown you that love cannot exist without jealousy, because, as I have already told you in more detail, jealousy between lovers is commended by every man who is experienced in love, while between husband and wife it is condemned throughout the world; the reason for this will be perfectly clear from a description of jealousy. Now jealousy is a true emotion whereby we greatly fear that the substance of our love may be weakened by some defect in serving the desires of our beloved, and it is an anxiety lest our love may not be returned.

"We find many, however, who are deceived in this matter and say falsely that a shameful suspicion is jealousy, just as many often make the mistake of saying that an alloy of silver and lead is the finest silver. Wherefore not a few being ignorant of the origin and description of jealousy, are often deceived and led into the gravest error. For even between persons who are not married this false jealousy may find a place and then they are no longer called 'lovers' but 'gentleman friend' and 'lady friend.' As for what you tried to prove by your answer—that the love which can be practiced without sin is far preferable—that, apparently, cannot stand. For whatever solaces married people extend to each other beyond what are inspired by the desire for offspring or the payment of the marriage debt, cannot be free from sin, and the punishment is always greater when the use of a holy thing is perverted by misuse than if we practice the ordinary abuses. It is a more serious offense in a wife than in another woman, for the too ardent lover, as we are taught by the apostolic law, is considered an adulterer with his own wife."

EIGHTH DIALOGUE

A man of the higher nobility speaks with a woman of the same class.

THE WOMAN SAYS: "I know that women should be the cause and origin of good things, that they should, of course, receive everybody with a joyful face and give him a courteous reception, and that they should speak to each one words appropriate to his condition and should clearly persuade every man to do courteous deeds and to avoid everything that has the appearance of boorishness and not to be so tenacious of his own property as to blacken his good name. But to show love is gravely to offend God and to prepare for many the perils of death. And besides it seems to bring innumerable pains to the lovers themselves and to cause them constant torments every day.

THE MAN SAYS: "If you choose to serve God alone, you must give up all worldly things and contemplate only the mysteries of the Heavenly Country, for God has not wished that anybody should keep his right foot on earth and his left foot in heaven, since no one can properly devote himself to the service of two masters. Now since it is clear that you have one foot on earth from the fact that you receive with a joyful countenance those who come to you and that you exchange courteous words with them and persuade them to do the works of love, I believe you would do better to enjoy love thoroughly than to lie to God under cloak of some pretense. I believe, however, that God cannot be seriously offended by love, for what is done under the compulsion of nature can be made clean by an easy expiation. Besides, it does not seem at all proper to class as a sin the thing from which the highest good in this life takes its origin and without which no man in the world could be considered worthy of praise.

"I want to explain to you something else that is in my mind, something which I know many keep hidden in their hearts, but which I do not think you are ignorant of, and that is that one kind of love is pure, and one is called mixed. It is the pure love which binds together the hearts of two lovers with feeling of delight. This kind consists in the contemplation of the mind and the affection of the heart; it goes as far as the kiss and the embrace and the modest contact with the nude lover, omitting the final solace, for that is not permitted to those who wish to love purely. This is the kind that anyone who is intent upon love ought to embrace with all his might, for this love goes on increasing without end, and we know that no one ever regretted practicing it, and the more of it one has the more one wants. This love is distinguished by being of such virtue that from it arises all excellence of character, and no injury comes from it, and God sees very little offense in it. No maiden can ever be corrupted by such a love, nor can a widow or a wife receive any harm or suffer any injury to her reputation. This love I cherish, this I follow and ever adore and never cease urgently to demand of you. But that is called mixed love which gets its effect from every delight of the flesh and culminates in the final act of Venus. What sort of love this is you may clearly see from what I have already said, for this kind quickly fails, and one often regrets having practiced it; by it one's neighbor is injured, the Heavenly King is offended, and from it come very grave dangers. But I do not say this as though I meant to condemn mixed love, I merely wish to show which of the two is preferable. But mixed love, too, is real love, and it is praiseworthy, and we say that it is the source of all good things, although from it grave dangers threaten, too. Therefore I approve of both pure love and mixed love, but I prefer to practice pure love. You should therefore put aside all fear of deception and choose one of the two kinds of love."

THE WOMAN SAYS: "From the replies that you have made to me, I know that you have had a great deal of experience in the art of love, so I am asking your opinion upon a certain matter connected with it. Now, since a certain woman of the most excellent character wished to reject one of her two suitors by letting him make his own choice, and to accept the other, she divided the solaces of love in her in this fashion. She said, 'Let one of you choose the upper half of me, and let the other suitor have the lower half.' Without a moment's delay each of them chose his part, and each insisted that he had chosen the better part, and argued that he was more worthy of her love than the other man was because he had chosen the worthier part. Since the woman I have mentioned did not wish to make a hasty decision she asked me, with the consent of the contenders, to give my decision as to which of them should be considered better in what he asked for. I therefore ask you which seems to you to have made the more praiseworthy choice."

THE MAN SAYS: "Since I am asking you for your love and you give me your pretext for not loving, you ought not to consider it discourteous of me if I try in every way to get rid of this excuse that is doing me the harm or to say something that will nullify it. Besides, you know that it will not take anything away from the rights of any lover if Your Prudence chooses to restrain my thoughtless acts. You should therefore be careful to do these things that you ought to do, because I shall never be separated from my determination to love you.

"You ask me, also, to give you my opinion on a matter on which no man of experience should hesitate, for who doubts that the man who chooses the solaces of the upper part should be preferred to the one who seeks the lower? For so far as the solaces of the lower part go, we are in no wise differentiated from brute beasts; but in this respect nature joins us to them. But the solaces of the upper part are, so to speak, attributes peculiar to the nature of man and are by this same nature denied to all the other animals. Therefore the unworthy man who chooses the lower part should be driven out from love just as though he were a dog, and he who chooses the upper part should be accepted as one who honors nature. Besides this, no man has ever been found who was tired of the solaces of the upper part, or satiated by practicing them, but the delight of the lower part quickly palls upon those who practice it, and it makes them repent of what they have done."

CHAPTER VI

The Love of the Clergy

Now, since in the preceding sections we have dealt with three classes of men: namely, commoners, simple nobility,